Kathy Furgang

EMMA WATSON

ACTRESS AND ACTIVIST

Enslow Publishing
101 W. 23rd Street
Suite 240
New York, NY 10011
USA
enslow.com

WORDS TO KNOW

audition To try out for a role.

campaign An organized plan to help meet a goal.

determined Having made a decision to work hard.

franchise A collection of films all based on one original work.

grueling Very difficult or demanding.

inspiration A positive influence that moves someone to do something.

radical Extreme.

United Nations An organization made up of many countries to promote peace and cooperation.

CONTENTS

Emma Watson

CHAPTER 1

EMMA AS A CHILD

Of the many actresses in Hollywood, Emma Watson is one of the most well-known and respected. She started her career as a beloved film character, Hermione Granger, based on the Harry Potter children's book series. But Emma is much more than just an actress. She is a person who works for human rights, especially the rights of women. Her fame as an actress has allowed her to play a much more important role in the real world.

When Emma was seven, she won a competition for reciting the James Reeves poem "The Sea." The poem compares the movement of the ocean to the moods and actions of a dog.

EARLY DAYS

Emma Charlotte Duerre Watson was born on April 15, 1990, in Paris, France. She grew up in England, in Oxfordshire. Both of Emma's parents are lawyers. They had a son, Alex, when Emma was three years old and then divorced when Emma was five.

Emma and her younger brother, Alex

Emma Says:

"I've always been like that; I give 100 percent. I can't do it any other way."

GROWING UP

When Emma was six years old, she realized that she wanted to become an actress. She loved singing, dancing, and performing. Her parents sent her to the Stagecoach Theatre Arts school in Oxford, England.

Although she loved acting and was learning about the craft, Emma had never acted professionally as a child. Despite her lack of experience, her theater teachers suggested that she be considered for a role in the upcoming film based on the best-selling Harry Potter series.

CHAPTER 2
THE HARRY POTTER YEARS

Emma **auditioned** for the role of Hermione Granger when she was nine. The Harry Potter series was very popular throughout England and the United States. The first book, *Harry Potter and the Sorcerer's Stone*, was about to be made into a full-length feature film. The filmmakers eventually turned the seven-part book series into an eight-part film series.

The story follows the youth of Harry Potter, a special wizard at the Hogwarts School of Witchcraft and Wizardry. Emma tried out for the role of one of Harry's closest friends, Hermione. She auditioned eight times before she finally landed the role!

The character of Hermione Granger was similar to the real personality of Harry Potter author J.K. Rowling. She wrote the role with herself in mind.

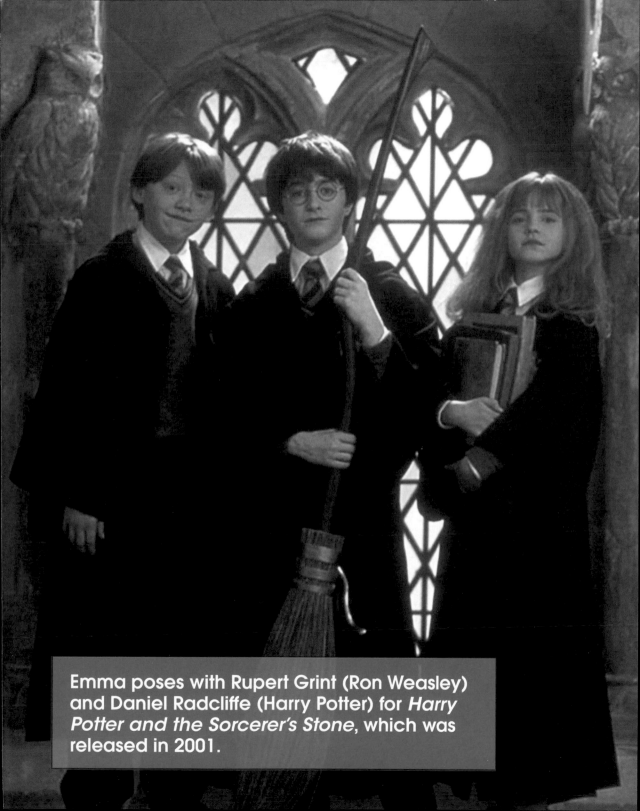

Emma poses with Rupert Grint (Ron Weasley) and Daniel Radcliffe (Harry Potter) for *Harry Potter and the Sorcerer's Stone*, which was released in 2001.

All grown up! The three *Harry Potter* stars attend a premiere in 2010.

THE JOURNEY TO THE BIG SCREEN

Getting the role in the Harry Potter films shot Emma to stardom. She went through a grueling schedule on the set. She worked hard on the first film. She had little time for anything except acting. The schedule was difficult for a young child.

Over the following years, Emma continued to work hard on the next seven films. Her work even became an inspiration to other girls. The character of Hermione was a leader. She was smart and **determined**. This helped other young girls to become strong in their own lives.

HARRY IS A HIT

The Harry Potter films were wildly successful. By the time the last film, *Harry Potter and the Deathly Hallows, Part 2*, had been released in 2011, the **franchise** was the most successful in film history. The books were one of the main reasons for this success. Kids around the world loved the Harry Potter book series and would wait desperately for the next book to be released. They had the same excitement waiting for each movie to come out.

Emma Says:

"Hermione is so close to who I am as a person that I never really had to research a role. I'm literally rediscovering what it means to be an actress."

While filming the series, the stars of the film grew from pre-teens to young adults. The whole time, Emma had continued to work on other films, such as *Ballet Shoes* in 2007, The *Tale of Despereaux* in 2008 and *My Week with Marilyn* in 2011. At the time of the last Harry Potter film, Emma had turned twenty-one years old. She was ready to move on to new projects.

Emma walks the red carpet at the British Fashion Awards in 2014.

Emma always had a great love for learning. As a teen, she did her schoolwork on the movie set. When it was time for college, she felt it was important to go, like other students her age. She attended Brown University in Rhode Island starting in 2009, and studied English literature.

LOOKING AHEAD

In 2011, Emma took the year off from school so she could focus on filming. She graduated in 2014. After graduation, she knew she wanted to do something important. She was very interested in women's equality

Brown University is one of the most competitive universities in the United States. It is one of eight schools that make up the Ivy League.

Emma beams at her graduation
from Brown University in 2014.

issues. While still in college, she had visited Bangladesh and Zambia to help promote education for girls.

WOMEN'S EQUALITY ISSUES

In 2014, Emma became a **United Nations** (UN) Women Goodwill Ambassador. The UN is an organization of many countries to help promote peace and cooperation around the world.

As part of her work with the UN, Emma helped start

Emma makes her voice heard at the 2017 Women's March on Washington.

Emma Says:
"Girls should never be afraid to be smart."

In 2014, Emma attended the launch of the HeForShe campaign at the United Nations, where she serves as UN Women Goodwill Ambassador.

MA WATSON

PRESIDENT GENERAL ASSEMBLY

a **campaign** called HeForShe. The campaign stresses the importance of men standing up for the rights of women. This, says the campaign, is a great way to fix the issue for everyone. On September 20, 2014, Emma made a speech in front of the United Nations about the issue of gender equality.

CHAPTER 4
A ROLE MODEL

Emma's speech at the United Nations made a big difference for a lot of people. This includes Nobel Peace Prize winner Malala Yousafzai. Malala is a young Pakistani woman who stands up for the right of girls and women to get an education. Because of this, she was shot by a **radical** group as a teen. She was a victim of the inequality that Emma describes in her campaign.

EMMA AND MALALA

When Malala heard Emma's speech to the United Nations, she was inspired. She thought about her own feelings about gender equality. She was most impressed with the words Emma spoke to try to get people involved. She said, "If not now, when? If not me, who?" The two met in 2015, when Emma interviewed Malala about her experiences and gender equality.

The 2015 film *He Named Me Malala* describes the life of Malala Yousafzai.

Malala Yousafzai and Emma met in 2015. The two activists share an interest in promoting education for girls and women.

Emma continues to pursue every project she takes on with dedication and passion.

Getting Inspired

As Emma continues to work for gender equality, she also continues to work as an actress. She chooses roles that inspire people to think about the world around them. Since the Harry Potter films, she has been in roles such as *The Perks of Being a Wallflower* and *Noah*. She also had a role as Belle in the live-action version of *Beauty and the Beast* and starred in the science fiction thriller *The Circle*.

Whether Emma's future projects include acting, activism, or both, she has many fans who are eager to see what she will do next.

Emma Says:

"All I can do is follow my instincts, because I'll never please everyone."

TIMELINE

1990 Emma Watson is born in Paris, France, on April 15.

1999 Emma lands the role of Hermione Granger in the Harry Potter films.

2001 The first Harry Potter film, *Harry Potter and the Sorcerer's Stone,* is released.

2009 Emma starts attending Brown University in Rhode Island.

2011 The last Harry Potter film, *Harry Potter and the Deathly Hallows, Part 2,* is released.

2014 Emma graduates from Brown University.

2014 She becomes a UN Women Goodwill Ambassador.

2015 Emma interviews Malala Yousafzai about gender equality.

2017 She wins MTV's Best Actor in a Movie Award for *Beauty and the Beast.*

BOOKS

Dellaccio, Tanya. *Emma Watson: Actress, Women's Rights Activist, and Goodwill Ambassador.* New York, NY: PowerKids Press, 2018.

Higgins, Nadia. *Emma Watson: From Wizards to Wallflowers* Minneapolis, MN: Lerner Publications, 2014.

Revenson, Jody. *J. K. Rowling's Wizarding World: Movie Magic Volume One.* Somerville, MA: Candlewick, 2016.

WEBSITES

Emma Watson

Emma-Watson.net

Enjoy photos, fun facts, and the latest news about Emma.

HeForShe

www.heforshe.org/en

Visit the website for the organization dedicated to gender equality. It was founded by UN Women and is operated in part by Emma Watson.

UN Women

www.unwomen.org/en

Visit the site for women that is part of the United Nations and their mission to improve the lives of women around the world.

INDEX

Published in 2019 by Enslow Publishing, LLC.
101 W. 23rd Street, Suite 240, New York, NY 10011

Library of Congress Cataloging-in-Publication Data

Names: Furgang, Kathy, author.
Title: Emma Watson : actress and activist / Kathy Furgang.
Description: New York, NY : Enslow Publishing, LLC., 2019. | Series: Junior biographies | Audience: Grades 3-6. | Includes bibliographical references and index.
Identifiers: LCCN 2017051693| ISBN 9780766097353 (library bound) | ISBN 9780766097360 (pbk.) | ISBN 9780766097377 (6 pack)
Subjects: LCSH: Watson, Emma, 1990–Juvenile literature. | Actors–Great Britain–Biography–Juvenile literature.
Classification: LCC PN2598.W25 F87 2019 | DDC 791.4302/8092 [B] –dc23
LC record available at https://lccn.loc.gov/2017051693

Printed in the United States of America

To Our Readers: We have done our best to make sure all website addresses in this book were active and appropriate when we went to press. However, the author and the publisher have no control over and assume no liability for the material available on those websites or on any websites they may link to. Any comments or suggestions can be sent by e-mail to customerservice@enslow.com.

Photos Credits: Cover, p. 1 Steve Granitz/Wire Image/Getty Images; p. 4 Kris Connor/FilmMagic/Getty Images; p. 6 Gregg DeGuire/Getty Images; p. 9 Collection Christophel/Alamy Stock Photo; p. 10 Dave Hogan/Getty Images; p. 12 Pascal Le Segretain/Getty Images; p. 14 © AP Images; p. 15 Theo Wargo/Getty Images; p. 16 Eduardo Munoz Alvarez/Getty Images; p. 19 KGC42/STAR MAX/IPx/AP; p. 20 Frazer Harrison/Getty Images; interior page bottoms (stars) Delpixel/Shutterstock.com.